WINERY DESIGN

teNeues

Editors and texts	Christian Datz, Christof Kullmann
Layout:	adk publishing, Mainz
Pre-press:	ScanComp, Wiesbaden
Translations:	SAW Communications, Dr. Sabine A. Werner, Mainz
	Dr. Suzanne Kirkbright (English), Nicoletta Negri (Italian),
	Céline Verschelde (French), Silvia Gómez de Antonio (Spanish)

Produced by adk publishing, Mainz
www.adk-publishing.de

Published by teNeues Publishing Group

teNeues Publishing Company
16 West 22nd Street, New York, NY 10010, USA
Tel.: 001-212-627-9090, Fax: 001-212-627-9511

teNeues Book Division
Kaistraße 18
40221 Düsseldorf, Germany
Tel.: 0049-211-994597-0, Fax: 0049-211-994597-40

teNeues Publishing UK Ltd.
P.O. Box 402
West Byfleet
KT14 7ZF, Great Britain
Tel.: 0044-1932-403509, Fax: 0044-1932-403514

teNeues France S.A.R.L.
4, rue de Valence
75005 Paris, France
Tel.: 0033-1-55 76 62 05, Fax: 0033-1-55 76 64 19

teNeues Ibérica S.L.
C/ Velázquez, 57 6.° izda.
28001 Madrid, Spain
Tel.: 0034-657-132 133

teNeues Representative Office Italy
Via San Vittore 36/1
20123 Milano, Italy
Tel.: 0039-347-76 40 55 1

www.teneues.com

ISBN-10:	3-8327-9106-X
ISBN-13:	978-3-8327-9106-3

© 2006 teNeues Verlag GmbH + Co. KG, Kempen

Printed in Italy

Bibliographic information published by Die Deutsche Bibliothek.
Die Deutsche Bibliothek lists this publication in the Deutsche Nationalbibliografie;
detailed bibliographic data is available in the Internet at http://dnb.ddb.de.

Content

**Introduction
Einleitung
Introduction
Introducción
Introduzione**

Wine and architecture—this ideal pairing has recently adopted a new profile. Whereas this couple used to conjure up images of luxurious "castle vineyards" in Bordeaux or Tuscany, nowadays, internationally, there is a host of ultramodern estate buildings and cellar facilities, which give winemaking a whole new look. True, the basic principles of wine production have hardly changed over the centuries, but the demands of operating a modern winery are essentially different to the traditional methods of the past.

This book features a representative selection of international wineries—ranging from small, traditional family wineries to impressive large-scale cellars, where the wine is produced virtually under industrial conditions. They share the common goal of striving for top quality products. The architectural concept can create essential conditions—this includes optimal stages of wine maturing as well as comprehensive control over temperature and humidity in the cellars. For many winemakers, being environmentally conscious and using sustainable techniques is also becoming increasingly important. Last not least, the external appearance of the estate buildings plays quite a special role, as ideally the wine quality is reflected in the winery's architecture.

Wein und Architektur – dieses Begriffspaar hat in den letzten Jahren eine neue Bedeutung erlangt. Dachte man dabei früher an luxuriöse „Weinschlösser" im Bordeaux oder in der Toskana, findet sich heute weltweit eine Vielzahl an hochmodernen Gutsgebäuden und Kelleranlagen, die dem Weinbau ein völlig neues Image geben. Zwar haben sich die grundlegenden Prinzipien der Weinherstellung über die Jahrhunderte kaum verändert, die Anforderungen an einen modernen Weingutsbetrieb unterscheiden sich jedoch wesentlich von den traditionellen Arbeitsweisen der Vergangenheit.

Dieser Band zeigt eine repräsentative Auswahl internationaler Weingüter – das Spektrum reicht von kleinen, traditionsbewussten Familienbetrieben bis hin zu beeindruckenden Großkellereien, bei denen der Wein unter nahezu industriellen Bedingungen hergestellt wird. Allen gemeinsam ist das Streben nach der höchsten Qualität ihrer Erzeugnisse. Das architektonische Konzept kann hierfür wesentliche Voraussetzungen schaffen – dazu gehören optimierte Arbeitsabläufe innerhalb der Produktion ebenso wie die umfassende Kontrolle über Temperatur und Feuchtigkeit in den Kellerräumen. Für viele Winzer gewinnt zudem das Bewusstsein für umwelt- und ressourcenschonende Arbeitsweisen immer mehr an Bedeutung, und nicht zuletzt spielt die äußere Erscheinung der Gebäude eine ganz besondere Rolle, soll sich in der Architektur des Weingutes doch die Qualität des Weines widerspiegeln.

Le vin et l'architecture : ces deux termes ont acquis une nouvelle signification au cours de ces dernières années. S'ils évoquaient autrefois des châteaux luxueux dans la région du Bordeaux ou en Toscane, ils font aujourd'hui allusion à une multitude de domaines ultramodernes et de caves dans le monde entier qui donnent une image tout à fait différente de la culture viticole. S'il est certain que les principes fondamentaux de la production du vin n'ont quasiment pas changé au cours des siècles, les exigences d'une entreprise viticole moderne se différencient toutefois nettement des modes de travail traditionnels du passé.

Cet ouvrage présente une sélection représentative de domaines viticoles internationaux, des petites entreprises familiales traditionnelles aux grandes caves imposantes dans lesquelles le vin est produit dans des conditions quasiment industrielles. Elles ont toutes en commun la recherche d'une qualité extrêmement élevée pour leurs produits. Le concept architectural peut créer des conditions essentielles : il influence notamment le processus de travail optimisé au cours de la production ainsi que le contrôle complet de la température et de l'humidité dans les caves. En outre, de nombreux vignerons privilégient de plus en plus des procédés respectant l'environnement et les ressources naturelles, sans oublier l'apparence extérieure des bâtiments qui joue un rôle très particulier : la qualité du vin est censée se refléter dans l'architecture du domaine viticole.

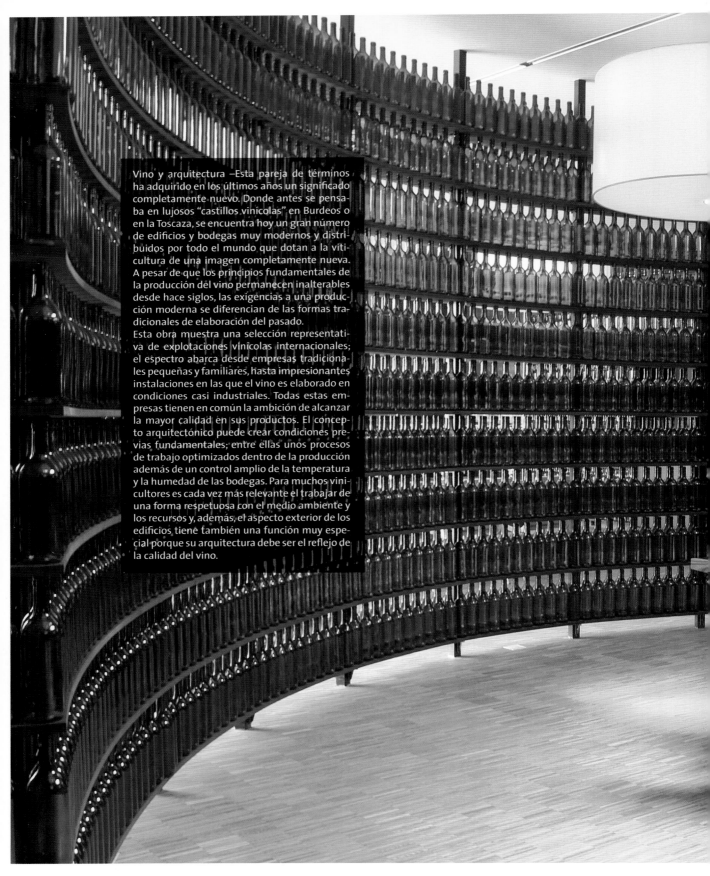

Vino y arquitectura —Esta pareja de términos ha adquirido en los últimos años un significado completamente nuevo. Donde antes se pensaba en lujosos "castillos vinícolas" en Burdeos o en la Toscaza, se encuentra hoy un gran número de edificios y bodegas muy modernos y distribuidos por todo el mundo que dotan a la viticultura de una imagen completamente nueva. A pesar de que los principios fundamentales de la producción del vino permanecen inalterables desde hace siglos, las exigencias a una producción moderna se diferencian de las formas tradicionales de elaboración del pasado.

Esta obra muestra una selección representativa de explotaciones vinícolas internacionales; el espectro abarca desde empresas tradicionales pequeñas y familiares, hasta impresionantes instalaciones en las que el vino es elaborado en condiciones casi industriales. Todas estas empresas tienen en común la ambición de alcanzar la mayor calidad en sus productos. El concepto arquitectónico puede crear condiciones previas fundamentales; entre ellas unos procesos de trabajo optimizados dentro de la producción además de un control amplio de la temperatura y la humedad de las bodegas. Para muchos vinicultores es cada vez más relevante el trabajar de una forma respetuosa con el medio ambiente y los recursos y, además, el aspecto exterior de los edificios tiene también una función muy especial porque su arquitectura debe ser el reflejo de la calidad del vino.

Vino e architettura, un binomio che negli ultimi anni ha assunto un nuovo significato: se prima vi si associavano lussuosi "castelli del vino" nella zona del Bordeaux o in Toscana, oggi in tutto il mondo c'è una moltitudine di modernissime case padronali e cantine che conferiscono alla viticoltura un'immagine completamente nuova. I principi di base della vinificazione sono rimasti pressoché invariati nel corso dei secoli, ma ciò che ci si aspetta da un'azienda vinicola moderna differisce considerevolmente dai metodi tradizionali del passato.

Questo volume propone una scelta rappresentativa di cantine internazionali, dalle piccole aziende familiari consce della propria tradizione alle imponenti grandi cantine in cui la produzione è stata fortemente razionalizzata. Tutte sono accomunate dal fatto che aspirano a raggiungere la massima qualità dei prodotti. Il progetto architettonico può fornire le premesse determinanti per ottenere tale scopo, come processi ottimizzati durante la produzione e il monitoraggio completo della temperatura e dell'umidità nelle cantine. Per moti produttori inoltre assume un'importanza sempre maggiore la sensibilità per metodi rispettosi dell'ambiente e delle risorse naturali, e non da ultimo anche l'aspetto degli edifici riveste un ruolo particolare, con l'intenzione che la qualità del vino si rispecchi nell'architettura delle tenute vinicole.

Canada

Mission Hill Family Estate Winery

Jackson-Triggs Niagara Estate

USA

Byron Vineyard and Winery

Dominus Estate

Quintessa

Roshambo Winery

France

Domaine Les Aurelles

Domaine Les Pierres Plantées

Domaine de Chevalier

Spain

Juan Alcorta

Bodegas Ysios

Viña Real

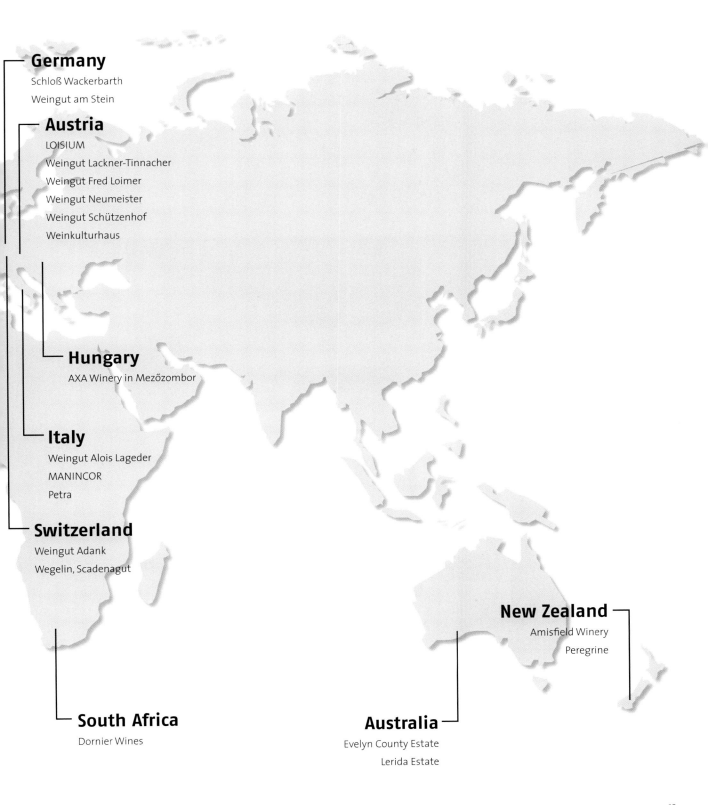

Germany

Schloß Wackerbarth

Weingut am Stein

Austria

LOISIUM

Weingut Lackner-Tinnacher

Weingut Fred Loimer

Weingut Neumeister

Weingut Schützenhof

Weinkulturhaus

Hungary

AXA Winery in Mezőzombor

Italy

Weingut Alois Lageder

MANINCOR

Petra

Switzerland

Weingut Adank

Wegelin, Scadenagut

New Zealand

Amisfield Winery

Peregrine

South Africa

Dornier Wines

Australia

Evelyn County Estate

Lerida Estate

13

Mission Hill Family Estate Winery

1730 Mission Hill Road · Westbank · British Columbia · Canada · www.missionhillwinery.com

2001
Olson Sundberg Kundig Allen Architects
www.olsonsundberg.com

Like a medieval castle or monastery estate, the winery rests majestically on a hill above Lake Okanagan. But the modern origin of the architecture is revealed in the details: at the winery's entrance, the impressive arch construction consists of two concrete elements, which are linked by a handcrafted stone block.

Wie eine mittelalterliche Burg- oder Kloster-anlage thront das Weingut auf einem Hügel oberhalb des Lake Okanagan. In den Details offenbart die Architektur jedoch ihren modernen Ursprung: So besteht die eindrucks-volle Bogenkonstruktion am Eingang des Weingutes aus zwei Betonformen, die durch einen handbearbeiteten Steinblock verbun-den werden.

Tel un château ou un cloître du Moyen Âge, ce domaine viticole trône sur une colline sur-plombant le Lake Okanagan. Les détails de son architecture traduisent cependant son origine moderne : la construction spectacu-laire de l'arc à l'entrée du domaine viticole est composée de deux moulages en béton qui ont été réunis par un bloc en pierre tra-vaillé à la main.

Como si fuera un castillo o un monasterio esta explotación vinícola corona la cima de una colina cercana al Lago Okanagan. Los de-talles nos descubren, sin embargo, unos orí-genes modernos: la impresionante arcada en la entrada de estas instalaciones se compo-ne de dos cuerpos de hormigón que se unen a través de un bloque de piedra artesanal.

La tenuta troneggia come un castello o un convento medievale su una collina che sovrasta il Lago Okanagan. Ma nei dettagli l'architettura svela la propria origine moder-na: l'imponente arco all'entrata della tenuta è costituito da due forme di calcestruzzo col-legate da un blocco di pietra scolpito a mano.

Jackson-Triggs Niagara Estate

2145 Regional Road 55 · Niagara-on-the-Lake · Ontario · Canada · www.jacksontriggswinery.com

2001
KPMB Kuwabara Payne McKenna Blumberg Architects
www.kpmb.com

Jackson Triggs is distinguished from other neighboring wineries by its emphatically modern construction. With its wooden-frame roof and the use of local natural stone, the building also incorporates elements typical for the region. Large sliding gates enable the two-storey entrance hall to be completely opened out.

Durch seine ausgesprochen moderne Bauweise unterscheidet sich Jackson Triggs von den anderen Weingütern der Umgebung. Mit seinem hölzernen Dachtragwerk und der Verwendung von örtlichem Naturstein bezieht der Bau jedoch auch regional typische Elemente ein. Die zweigeschossige Eingangshalle kann durch große Schiebetore vollständig geöffnet werden.

Jackson Triggs se distingue des autres domaines viticoles de la région par son mode de construction extrêmement moderne. L'édifice intègre toutefois également des éléments typiques de la région avec sa charpente en bois et le recours à la pierre naturelle locale. De grandes portes coulissantes permettent d'ouvrir entièrement le hall d'entrée conçu sur deux étages.

Jackson Triggs se diferencia de las demás explotaciones vinícolas de la zona por su moderna arquitectura. Sin embargo, la estructura portante de su tejado realizada en madera y el empleo de piedra natural del lugar son también conexiones con los típicos elementos regionales. El vestíbulo, de dos alturas, puede abrirse completamente a través de dos grandes puertas correderas.

Grazie all'architettura decisamente moderna Jackson Triggs si distingue dalle altre aziende vinicole della zona. La costruzione integra però anche elementi tipici della regione, presenti nelle travi in legno che sostengono il tetto e nell'impiego di pietra naturale locale. L'entrata, allestita su due piani, può venire aperta completamente spostando i portoni scorrevoli.

Byron Vineyard and Winery

5250 Tepusquet Road · Santa Maria · California · USA · www.byronwines.com

1996
Johnson Fain Partners
www.jfpartners.com

The winery's outer appearance looks a little unspectacular. By contrast, the interiors are spacious and carefully designed—including the impressive foyer and tasting room, with its generous skylight, as well as winemaking facilities and barrels located above ground.

Das äußere Erscheinungsbild des Weingutes wirkt eher unspektakulär. Die Innenräume hingegen sind großzügig und sorgfältig gestaltet – dazu zählen das eindrucksvolle Foyer und der Degustationsraum mit seinem großen Oberlicht ebenso wie die Produktionsanlagen und die oberirdischen Fasskeller.

L'apparence extérieure du domaine viticole n'est pas vraiment spectaculaire. Les pièces intérieures sont en revanche généreuses et agencées avec soin : le foyer impressionnant, la salle de dégustation avec sa grande imposte ainsi que les installations de production et les chais en surface.

La imagen exterior de esta explotación vinícola no es muy espectacular. En cambio, los espacios interiores son amplios y están decorados con mucho detalle; a estas estancias pertenece el vestíbulo y el centro de degustación, con su gran claraboya, además de las instalaciones de la producción y la bodega de barriles de superficie.

L'aspetto esterno dell'azienda è piuttosto sobrio. Gli interni invece sono ampi e accurati – comprendono un imponente foyer e un locale degustazioni con un grande lucernario, gli impianti di produzione e una barricaia non sotterranea.

Dominus Estate

2570 Napanook Road · Yountville · California · USA · www.dominusestate.com

1997
Herzog & deMeuron

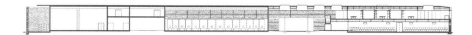

The external walls of what initially appears as a simple structure are made of so-called gabions—rectangular wire baskets, which are normally used as supporting walls in agricultural construction. These wire baskets are filled with different quarry stone from the immediate vicinity of the winery. A quirky texture is created that perfectly harmonizes with the landscape.

Die Außenwände des auf den ersten Blick einfachen Baukörpers bestehen aus so genannten Gabionen – rechtwinkligen Drahtkörben, die sonst eher als Stützwände im Landschaftsbau verwendet werden. Diese Drahtkörbe sind mit unterschiedlichen Bruchsteinen aus der unmittelbaren Umgebung des Weingutes gefüllt. So entsteht eine eigenwillige Textur, die sich perfekt in die Landschaft einfügt.

Les parois extérieures de l'édifice, dont la construction paraît simple au premier coup d'œil, sont composées de gabions, muselets rectangulaires plutôt utilisés comme parois de soutien dans l'architecture paysagiste. Ces muselets sont remplis de différents moellons provenant directement de la région du domaine viticole, créant ainsi une texture originale qui se fond à merveille dans le paysage.

Las paredes exteriores de esta construcción a primera vista sencilla, se componen de los llamados gabiones; grandes cajas rectangulares de alambre que habitualmente se emplean como paredes de soporte en las construcciones del campo. Estos cestos de alambre están rellenados con diferentes piedras de cantera de los alrededores. De este modo se crea una textura caprichosa que adapta perfectamente al paisaje.

Le pareti esterne di questa costruzione apparentemente semplice sono costituite da cosiddetti gabbioni, parallelepipedi di filo di ferro di solito impiegati come sostegni nelle opere di ingegneria naturalistica. I gabbioni sono stati riempiti con pietre di cava di differenti tipi provenienti dalle immediate vicinanze, generando una struttura originale che si integra perfettamente nel paesaggio.

Quintessa

1601 Silverado Trail · Rutherford · California · USA · www.quintessa.com

2003
Walker Warner Architects
www.walker-warner.com

A distinctive, crescent-shaped natural stonewall, situated on the periphery of a small hill, influences the winery's exterior image. To the rear, production and cellar facilities are concealed underground. On the site's roof is a visitor center for tasting and wine sales, where visitors are immersed in a distinctly refined, lounge-style atmosphere.

Eine markante, sichelförmige Naturstein-wand am Rande eines kleinen Hügels prägt den äußeren Eindruck des Weingutes. Dahinter verbergen sich unterirdische Produktions- und Kellerräume. Auf dem Dach der Anlage befindet sich ein Besucherzentrum für die Verkostung und den Verkauf der Weine, in dem den Besucher eine ausgesprochen edle, loungeartige Atmosphäre umgibt.

En forme de faucille et en pierre naturelle, le mur original situé le long d'une petite colline détermine l'image que le domaine viticole donne à l'extérieur. Derrière ce mur sont dissimulées des salles de production et des caves souterraines. Un centre destiné à la dégustation et à la vente des vins, dans lequel le visiteur est plongé dans une atmosphère très chic et lounge, a été installé sur le toit de l'ensemble.

Una destacada pared de piedra natural en forma de hoz en el borde de una pequeña colina marca la impresión exterior de la explotación vinícola. Detrás de este muro se esconden los espacios subterráneos de la producción y de la bodega. En el techo de la instalación se encuentra un centro para visitantes donde se pueden degustar y adquirir los vinos en un ambiente extraordinariamente elegante y similar a un lounge.

Un'appariscente parete in pietra naturale a forma di falce alle pendici di una collina caratterizza l'aspetto esteriore dell'azienda. Dietro ad essa si celano cantine e locali per la produzione sotterranei. Sul tetto della struttura è stato costruito un centro visitatori, per la degustazione e la vendita dei vini, in un'atmosfera lounge, particolarmente ricercata.

Roshambo Winery

3000 Westside Road · Healdsburg · California · USA · www.roshambowinery.com

2002
Jaques Ullmann & Thomas Johnson

The winery's buildings are situated above the vineyards at the edge of Russian River Valley. The visitors' center is utilized not only for sales and wine tasting, but also as an art gallery. The linear wooden structure of the ceiling's cladding emphasizes the elegant curve of the roof construction.

Die Gebäude des Weingutes liegen oberhalb der Weinberge am Rande des Russian River Valley. Das Besucherzentrum dient neben dem Verkauf und der Degustation der Weine auch als Kunstgalerie. Die lineare Holzstruktur der Deckenverkleidung unterstreicht den eleganten Schwung der Dachkonstruktion.

Les bâtiments du domaine viticole sont situés au-dessus des vignes, le long de la Russian River Valley. Le centre pour les visiteurs, destiné à la dégustation et à la vente des vins, sert également de galerie d'art. La structure linéaire du bois du coffrage du plafond souligne la ligne élégante de la construction du toit.

Los edificios de la propiedad vinícola están ubicados por encima de los viñedos en la linde del Russian River Valley. El centro para visitantes, además de ser un lugar para la venta y degustación de los vinos, también hace las veces de galería de arte. La estructura lineal de madera del revestimiento del techo subraya el elegante alzado de la construcción del tejado.

Gli edifici della tenuta sovrastano i vigneti al margine della Russian River Valley. Il centro visitatori, adibito alla vendita e degustazione dei vini, funge anche da galleria d'arte. La struttura lineare del soffitto di legno sottolinea l'elegante forma ondulata del tetto.

Juan Alcorta

Camino de Lapuebla 50 · Logroño · La Rioja · Spain · www.bodegasjuanalcorta.com

2003
Ignacio Quemada Architect

In the vast winemaking and cellar facilities in the north east of Spain, wine is stored in excess of 70,000 oak barrels and 6 million bottles. The architects succeeded in over-accentuating the site's industrial character in the design. Wood and colored concrete are predominant design features in the functional, but impressively staged cellars.

In den riesigen Produktions- und Kellergebäuden im Nordosten Spaniens lagern über 70.000 Eichenholzfässer und 6 Millionen Flaschen Wein. Den Architekten gelang es, den industriellen Charakter der Anlage gestalterisch zu überhöhen. In den funktionalen, aber dennoch eindrucksvoll inszenierten Kellerräumen dominieren Holz und gefärbter Beton als Gestaltungsmittel.

Dans les immenses salles de production et les caves du Nord-Est de l'Espagne, plus de 70 000 tonneaux en bois de chêne et 6 millions de bouteilles de vin sont stockés. Les architectes ont réussi à dissimuler le caractère industriel de l'ensemble grâce aux matériaux privilégiés : le bois et le béton coloré dominent dans ces caves qui sont fonctionnelles, mais toutefois mises en scène de manière surprenante.

En los gigantescos edificios de la producción y de las bodegas situadas en el nordeste de España hay almacenados más de 70.000 cubas de madera de haya y 6 millones de botellas de vino. Los arquitectos subrayar el carácter industrial de la instalación desde el punto de vista creativo. En los espacios de la bodega, funcionales aunque escenificados de forma efectista, los principales elementos decorativos son la madera y el hormigón coloreado.

In questi enormi edifici adibiti alla produzione e a cantina situati nel Nordest della Spagna si trovano oltre 70.000 botti di rovere e 6 milioni di bottiglie di vino. Gli architetti sono riusciti a conferire un aspetto speciale al carattere industriale del complesso. Nelle cantine, funzionali ma ciononostante spettacolari, gli elementi progettuali predominanti sono il legno e il calcestruzzo colorato.

Bodegas Ysios

Camino de la Hoya, s/n · Laguardia · Álava · Rioja · Spain · www.bodegasysios.com

2001
Santiago Calatrava
www.calatrava.com

The Bodegas Ysios is located as a powerful, monumental sculpture in the middle of an equally impressive landscape. A link between the environment and construction is supposed to be created not by the transparent façades, but by the dynamic form-language of the curving walls and roofs.

Als kraftvolle, monumentale Skulptur steht die Bodegas Ysios inmitten einer ebenso beeindruckenden Landschaft. Eine Verbindung zwischen Umgebung und Bauwerk soll nicht durch transparente Fassaden, sondern durch die bewegte Formensprache der geschwungenen Wände und Dächer entstehen.

Sculpture vigoureuse et monumentale, la Bodegas Ysios est située au milieu d'un paysage tout aussi impressionant. Le lien entre l'environnement et l'édifice n'a pas été créé par des façades transparentes, mais par la forme courbée des murs et les toits arqués.

La bodega Ysios se levanta como una escultura enérgica y monumental en medio de un paisaje igual de impresionante. La conexión entre el entorno y el edificio no se establece a través de las fachadas transparentes sino con el animado lenguaje formal de las paredes y los tejados ondulados.

Bodegas Ysios sta come una scultura vigorosa e monumentale nel bel mezzo di un affascinante paesaggio. Il legame fra la costruzione e la natura circostante non viene instaurato mediante facciate trasparenti, bensì attraverso il movimentato linguaggio formale di pareti e tetti arcuati.

Viña Real

Ctra. Logroño · Laguardia · Álava · Rioja · Spain · www.cvne.com

2004
Philippe Mazières

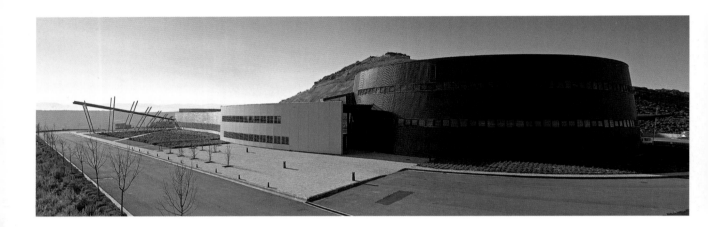

This winery's main building is meant to be reminiscent of a vast wooden barrel, where ultra-modern production facilities are concealed on two levels. Two vast pipes were tunneled into the rock for optimal wine storage.

An ein riesiges Holzfass soll der Hauptbau dieses Weingutes erinnern, in dem sich auf zwei Ebenen hochmoderne Produktionsanlagen verbergen. Zur optimalen Lagerung des Weines wurden zwei riesige Tunnelröhren in den Fels getrieben.

La construction principale de ce domaine viticole est censée rappeler un immense tonneau en bois dans lequel se cachent des installations de production ultramodernes sur deux étages. Deux gigantesques tunnels ont été creusés dans le rocher afin de permettre un stockage optimal du vin.

El edificio principal de esta explotación vinícola evoca a una gigantesca cuba de madera en la que se ocultan las instalaciones de producción altamente modernas repartidas en dos pisos. Para el almacenamiento óptimo del vino se han instalado dos gigantescas cañerías que atraviesan la montaña.

L'edificio principale di quest'azienda vinicola, in cui si trovano modernissimi impianti di produzione disposti su due piani, ricorda un'enorme botte di legno. Per la conservazione ottimale del vino si sono scavate nella roccia due enormi gallerie.

Domaine Les Aurelles

Les Vignals · Nizas · Languedoc-Roussillon · France

2001
perraudin architectes
Olivier Schertenleib · Elisabeth Polzella
www.perraudinarchitectes.com

Large cuboids made of sand-lime bricks shape this long stretch of building. Due to its perpendicular position in relation to the mountain slope, the building's northern sector is sunk into the site as a wine cellar. Offices and storage rooms are located in the building's southern sector. Diffused daylight reaches the estate's interior rooms through a narrow strip of light below the ceiling.

Große Quader aus Kalksandstein formen diesen lang gestreckten Baukörper. Durch seine Lage senkrecht zum Hang versinkt der nördliche Gebäudeteil als Weinkeller im Gelände. Im südlichen Abschnitt des Gebäudes befinden sich die Büros und Lagerräume. Durch ein schmales Lichtband unterhalb der Decke gelangt diffuses Tageslicht in die Innenräume der Anlage.

De grands parallélépipèdes rectangles en grès calcaire forment le corps du bâtiment qui s'étend en longueur. Son emplacement vertical par rapport au versant fait disparaître la partie nord du bâtiment dans le terrain et en fait une cave à vin. Les bureaux et les pièces de stockage sont situés dans la partie sud du bâtiment. La lumière du jour diffuse parvient dans les pièces intérieures de l'ensemble à travers un bandeau de lumière étroit placé sous le plafond.

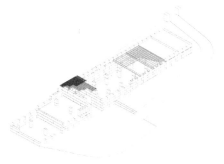

Este edificio alargado está compuesto de grandes rectángulos de piedra caliza. Por su posición vertical a la pendiente, la parte norte del edificio está excavada en el terreno y ella se ha situado la bodega. En el ala sur se encuentran los despachos y las instalaciones de almacenamiento. La estrecha abertura longitudinal por debajo del techo permite el paso de luz del día difusa a los espacios interiores.

Grandi blocchi di arenaria calcarea formano questa costruzione longitudinale. Con la sua posizione verticale rispetto al pendio la parte nord dell'edificio sprofonda nel terreno ed è adibita a cantina. La parte sud ospita gli uffici e i magazzini. Attraverso una lunga fascia di finestre appena sotto il soffitto penetra nei locali luce diurna diffusa.

Domaine Les Pierres Plantées

Chemin des Salines · Vauvert · Languedoc-Roussillon · France

1997
perraudin architectes
www.perraudinarchitectes.com

The winery was made out of giant sand-lime bricks, joined together to form a structure as simple as it is impressive. The giant bulk of the stone cuboids and a skilful cooling system guarantee optimal conditions in the interior for wine production and storage, even during the summer months.

Das Weingut wurde aus riesigen Kalksandsteinblöcken zu einem ebenso einfachen wie eindrucksvollen Bauwerk zusammengefügt. Die enorme Masse der Steinquader und ein geschicktes Belüftungssystem sorgen in den Innenräumen auch in den Sommermonaten für optimale Produktions- und Lagerbedingungen.

Ce domaine viticole a été conçu à partir d'immenses blocs de grès calcaire afin de créer un édifice à la fois simple et imposant. La masse énorme des parallélépipèdes rectangles en pierre et le système d'aération sophistiqué garantissent des conditions optimales de production et de stockage dans les pièces intérieures, même pendant les mois d'été.

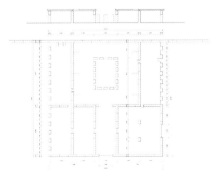

El edificio de la explotación vinícola se compone de gigantescos bloques de piedra caliza que le dan un aspecto sencillo pero también impresionante. La enorme masa de los bloques de piedra y un inteligente sistema de ventilación crean unas condiciones óptimas de producción y almacenamiento en los espacios interiores, también en verano.

Giganteschi blocchi di arenaria calcarea sono stati utilizzati per realizzare una costruzione che colpisce nonostante la sua semplicità. I massicci blocchi di pietra e un sistema di aerazione intelligente fanno sì che le condizioni produttive e di conservazione siano ottimali anche nei mesi estivi.

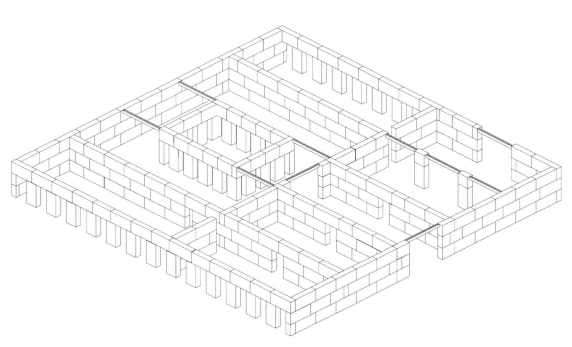

Domaine de Chevalier

Léognan · Bordeaux · France · www.domainedechevalier.com

1991
Hugues Legrix de la Salle

The winery is hidden away right in the middle of a pine forest on a clearing that measures up to 40 hectares. The new buildings stylistically harmonized with the historical 19th Century building elements. Stainless steel tanks for maturing the wine are arranged in a radial pattern and located in a striking rotunda.

Das Weingut liegt versteckt inmitten eines Kiefernwaldes auf einer gut 40 Hektar großen Lichtung. Die Neubauten wurden den historischen Gebäudeteilen aus dem 19. Jahrhundert stilistisch angepasst. In einer auffälligen Rotunde befinden sich die radial angeordneten Gärtanks aus Edelstahl.

Ce domaine viticole est caché au beau milieu d'une forêt de pins dans une grande clairière de 40 hectares. Le style des bâtiments récents a été adapté aux parties historiques datant du 19ème siècle. Les cuves en inox ont été mises en place radialement dans une rotonde qui ne passe pas inaperçue.

La explotación vinícola se oculta en un claro de 40 hectáreas dentro de un bosque de pinos. Los edificios nuevos se adaptaron al estilo de las construcciones históricas del siglo XIX. En una llamativa rotonda se ordenan radialmente los tanques de acero inoxidable.

La tenuta è nascosta in una pineta, in una radura di ben 40 ettari. Le nuove costruzioni sono state concepite in modo tale da armonizzare stilisticamente con il complesso storico risalente all'Ottocento. In un appariscente edificio rotondo si trovano disposte sulla circonferenza le vasche di fermentazione in acciaio inox.

Schloss Wackerbarth

Sächsisches Staatsweingut GmbH · Wackerbarthstraße 1 · Radebeul · Germany · www.schloss-wackerbarth.de

2002
h.e.i.z.Haus Architektur + Stadtplanung Partnerschaft · www.heizhaus.de
Haufe Lohse Pätzig Landschaftsarchitekten · www.hlp-dd.de

The architects have courageously paired up the Baroque buildings and garden facilities with a strictly modern design for the hall for wine and champagne production. The building's interior is defined by concrete, steel and laminated wood, but in selected areas, special materials such as laser veneering are used on the wooden panels refined surfaces.

Mutig haben die Architekten den barocken Gebäuden und Gartenanlagen eine konsequent modern gestaltete Produktionshalle für Wein und Sekt gegenübergestellt. Das Innere des Gebäudes wird durch Beton, Stahl und Leimholz bestimmt – in ausgewählten Bereichen jedoch wurden die Oberflächen durch besondere Materialien wie lasierte Furnierholztafeln veredelt.

Les architectes ont osé opposer les édifices et les jardins baroques à un hangar moderne destiné à la production du vin et du crémant. L'intérieur du bâtiment est déterminé par du béton, de l'acier et du bois collé. À certains endroits, les surfaces ont été toutefois revêtues de matériaux spéciaux comme des placages enduits d'une lasure.

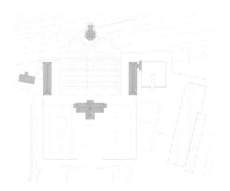

Los arquitectos se han atrevido a situar frente a los edificios barrocos y los jardines un pabellón de producción moderno para vino y champaña. El interior de esta construcción está determinado por el hormigón, el acero y la madera encolada; en espacios seleccionados, sin embargo, las superficies han sido ennoblecidas con materiales especiales como paneles de chapa de madera barnizados.

Gli architetti hanno avuto il coraggio di porre di fronte agli edifici e parchi barocchi un capannone assolutamente moderno adibito alla produzione di vino e spumante. Gli interni sono caratterizzati da calcestruzzo, acciaio e legno lamellare – in determinate zone le superfici sono state impreziosite con materiali particolari, come pannelli di legno impiallacciato finiti con vernice trasparente.

Weingut am Stein

Ludwig Knoll · Mittlerer Steinbergweg 5 · Würzburg · Franken · Germany · www.weingut-am-stein.de

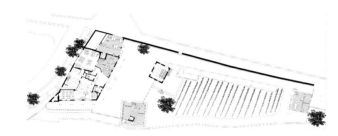

2005
hofmann keicher ring architekten
www.hofmann-keicher-ring.de

Complimentary to the estate's existing buildings, the "WeinWerk" was created as a special place for tastings, presentations and seminars. The unusual, multi-layered façade out of natural round timber with a layer of greenish glass behind transfers the color-fulness of the surrounding vineyards to the building's architecture.

Als Ergänzung zu den vorhandenen Gutsge-bäuden entstand mit dem „WeinWerk" ein besonderer Ort für Verkostungen, Präsenta-tionen und Seminare. Die ungewöhnliche, mehrschichtige Fassade aus naturbelasse-nen Rundhölzern und einer dahinter liegen-den Ebene aus grünlichem Glas überträgt die Farbigkeit der umgebenden Weinberge in die Architektur des Gebäudes.

Le « WeinWerk » fut créé dans le but de com-pléter le domaine existant. Il s'agit d'un lieu particulier où ont lieu les dégustations, les présentations et les séminaires. La façade inhabituelle en bois arrondi non traité et conçue en plusieurs couches et la coulisse en verre verdâtre projettent les couleurs des vignes environnantes sur l'architecture du bâtiment.

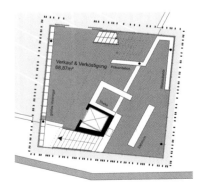

Complementando a los edificios de la explotación ya existentes se levantó el "WeinWerk" como un lugar especial para la degustación, la presentación y los semina-rios. La inusal fachada, de varias capas de listones redondeados de madera sin tratar y el nivel anterior de cristal verdoso traslada el colorido de las viñas a la arquitectura del edificio.

Per integrare gli edifici esistenti si è realiz-zato il "WeinWerk", un luogo particolare per degustazioni, presentazioni e corsi. L'insolita facciata multistrato, costituita da tondame non trattato con dietro uno strato di vetro verdastro, trasmette all'architettura dell'edi-ficio la colorazione dei vigneti circostanti.

Weingut Adank

Familie Hansruedi Adank · St. Luzi · Fläsch · Graubünden · Switzerland · www.adank-weine.ch

2001
atelier-f Kurt Hauenstein
www.atelier-f.ch

Instead of the old premises, this small extension was created for presentation and wine tasting. Window openings at irregular intervals produce an interesting, lively façade image and a charming, almost minimalist interior. The new building carries on below ground as an extension to existing cellar facilities.

Anstelle einer alten Remise entstand dieser kleine Anbau, der zur Präsentation und Verkostung der Weine dient. Unregelmäßig verteilte Fensteröffnungen erzeugen ein interessantes, lebendiges Fassadenbild und einen reizvollen, beinahe minimalistischen Innenraum. Unter der Erde setzt sich der Neubau in einer Erweiterung der vorhandenen Kelleranlage fort.

Cette petite annexe qui sert à la présentation et à la dégustation des vins a été installée à la place d'une ancienne remise. Les ouvertures des fenêtres, réparties de manière irrégulière, créent une façade intéressante et vivante ainsi qu'une pièce intérieure charmante, presque minimaliste. Le nouveau bâtiment continue sous terre et prolonge la cave existante.

Este pequeño edificio anexo que se levanta en el lugar que ocupaba una antigua cochera se emplea para la presentación y la degustación de los vinos. Las ventanas, repartidas de forma irregular, crean una fachada interesante y llena de vida y un espacio interior encantador casi minimalista. Debajo de la tierra se oculta el nuevo edificio continúa en una ampliación de la bodega ya existente.

Dove un tempo si trovava un'antica rimessa è sorto questo piccolo edificio annesso, adibito all'esposizione e degustazione dei vini. Finestre distribuite irregolarmente creano una facciata interessante e animata e un interno affascinante, quasi minimalistico. La parte interrata della nuova costruzione costituisce un ampliamento delle cantine preesistenti.

Wegelin, Scadenagut

Bothmarweg 1 · Malans · Graubünden · Switzerland · www.pwegelin.ch

2004
Konrad Erhard, Daniel Schwitter

Production and bottling plants are situated on the new building's two lower ground floors, along with an effectively illuminated Barrique cellar. The glass pavilion construction above accommodates the tasting room, offices and a kitchen. A panoramic vista over Chur's Rhine valley is available from the spacious terrace.

In den beiden unterirdischen Geschossen des Neubaus liegen die Produktions- und Abfüllanlagen sowie ein effektvoll beleuchteter Barriquekeller. Im darüber liegenden, gläsernen Pavillonbau sind der Degustationsraum, Büros und eine Küche untergebracht. Von der großzügigen Terrasse bietet sich ein weiter Blick über das Churer Rheintal.

Les deux étages souterrains du nouveau bâtiment hébergent les installations de production et de remplissage, ainsi qu'une cave de barriques fantastiquement éclairée. Dans le pavillon en verre situé au-dessus se trouvent la salle de dégustation, les bureaux et une cuisine. On peut admirer de la terrasse généreuse une superbe vue sur la Vallée rhénane du Chur.

Los dos niveles subterráneos de esta nueva construcción albergan las instalaciones de producción y de embotellado, además de una bodega de barriles iluminada con efectismo. En el pabellón acristalado situado encima se encuentran los espacios para la degustación, los despachos y una cocina. Desde la amplia terraza se extiende una vista sobre el Valle del Rin de Chur.

Nei due piani interrati del nuovo edificio si trovano gli impianti per la produzione e l'imbottigliamento e una barricaia con illuminazione di grande effetto. Sopra, il padiglione in vetro ospita il locale degustazioni, gli uffici e una cucina. Dall'ampia terrazza si gode il panorama della valle del Reno presso Chur.

LOISIUM

Visitors' Center · Loisiumallee 1 · Langenlois · Niederösterreich · Austria · www.loisium.at

2003
LOISIUM Visitors' Center: Steven Holl Architects · www.stevenholl.com
LOISIUM Kellerwelten: Steiner Sarnen Schweiz · www.steinersarnenschweiz.ch

Visitors at LOISIUM are introduced to the subject of wine in a sensual and informative way by taking the underground tour covering about one km. This includes the old wine cellars, dating back nine centuries, as well as an ultra-modern winemaking facility. The exterior shell of the imposing reception building consists of brushed aluminum; and large sections of the interior wall surfaces were covered with a layer of light cork.

Auf einem unterirdischen Rundgang von knapp einem km Länge wird den Besuchern des LOISIUMS das Thema Wein auf sinnliche und informative Weise präsentiert. Dazu gehören 900 Jahre alte Gewölbekeller ebenso wie eine hochmoderne Produktionsanlage. Die Außenhaut des imposanten Empfangsgebäudes besteht aus gebürstetem Aluminium, große Teile der Wandoberflächen im Inneren wurden mit hellem Kork beschichtet.

En un recorrido subterráneo de casi un km de longitud, el mundo del vino se presenta a los visitantes de LOISIUM de una forma sensorial e informativa. Este pase incluye la bodega de techos abovedados de 900 años de antigüedad y una moderna instalación productora. La piel exterior del impresionante edificio de recepción está compuesta por aluminio cepillado y gran parte de las superficies de las paredes interiores están revestidas con corcho.

C'est au cours d'une visite souterraine de près d'un km de long que les visiteurs du LOISIUM peuvent découvrir le monde du vin de maniére sensuelle et informative. Des caves voûtées datant de 900 ans ainsi qu'une installation de production ultramoderne en font partie. La paroi externe de l'imposant bâtiment de réception est composée d'aluminium brossé ; de grandes parties des surfaces murales intérieures ont été dotées d'un revêtement en liège clair.

In un percorso sotterraneo lungo poco meno di un chilometro il mondo del vino viene presentato ai visitatori del LOISIUM in modo informativo e coinvolgendo con tutti i sensi. Ne fanno parte cantine a volta risalenti a 900 anni fa e anche un impianto di produzione all'avanguardia. La struttura esterna dell'imponente centro di accoglienza è in alluminio spazzolato, mentre all'interno gran parte della superficie delle pareti è rivestita in sughero.

Weingut Lackner-Tinnacher

Fritz + Wilma Tinnacher · Steinbach 12 · Gamlitz · Steiermark · Austria · www.tinnacher.at

2003
Rolf Rauner · www.architektur-rauner.at
breitenthaler · www.breitenthaler.at

The winery's new cellar for wine barrels and storage tanks was built into the mountainside as a reinforced concrete structure. Thanks to the wooden-slats on the cladding and lush plants on the roof, the site harmoniously integrates with its surroundings in spite of its distinctive, cubic shape.

Der neue Fass- und Tankkeller des Weingutes wurde als Stahlbeton-Konstruktion in den Hang hineingebaut. Durch eine Verkleidung aus Holzlatten und ein begrüntes Dach integriert sich die Anlage trotz ihrer markanten, kubischen Form harmonisch in die Umgebung.

Les nouveaux chais du domaine viticole sont une construction en béton et en acier qui a été intégrée dans le versant. Grâce au revêtement en lattes de bois et au toit végétalisé, l'ensemble se marie harmonieusement avec l'environnement malgré sa forme cubique surprenante.

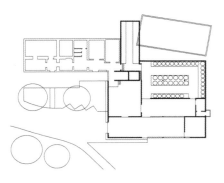

La nueva bodega de las cubas y de los tanques de esta explotación vinícola, una construcción de acero y hormigón, fue excavada en la pendiente. A pesar de su marcada forma cubista, el edificio se integra con armonía en su entorno gracias a su revestimiento de listones de madera y a su tejado cubierto con plantas.

La nuova cantina della tenuta, che ospita le botti e le vasche, è una struttura in calcestruzzo armato seminterrata realizzata sul pendio della collina. Grazie a un rivestimento in assi di legno e al tetto a verde lo stabilimento si integra armoniosamente nel paesaggio nonostante l'appariscente forma cubica.

Weingut Fred Loimer

Haindörfer Vögerlweg 23 · Langenlois · Niederösterreich · Austria · www.loimer.at

2000
Andreas Burghardt
www.burghardt.co.at

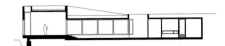

The building's impact as a black, monolithic structure is located on the site of an 18th Century wine cellar. The historic vaults were carefully exposed and restored, with a radically designed new structure created above it, where a glass wine tasting table, measuring 8 meters long, acts as a focal point and eye-catching feature.

Der schwarze, monolithisch wirkende Baukörper steht auf einem Keller aus dem 18. Jahrhundert. Die historischen Gewölbe wurden sorgsam freigelegt und restauriert, darüber entstand ein radikal gestalteter Neubau, in dem ein 8 Meter langer, gläserner Degustationstisch als Zentrum und Blickfang dient.

Tel un monolithe, le corps noir du bâtiment a été placé au-dessus de la cave du 18ème siècle. Les voûtes historiques ont été soigneusement mises à jour et restaurées. Un bâtiment neuf à l'agencement radical, dans lequel une longue table de dégustation en verre de 8 mètres de long attire le regard, a été construit au-dessus.

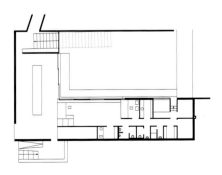

El edificio negro y de aspecto monolítico se levanta sobre una bodega del siglo XVIII. Las bóvedas históricas se descubrieron y restauraron y, por encima, se levantó un edificio de diseño radical cuyo centro de atención es la mesa de degustación de cristal de 8 metros de longitud.

La costruzione nera, dall'aspetto monolitico, sorge su una cantina del Settecento. Le antiche volte sono state messe allo scoperto e restaurate con cura, e sopra di esse si è costruito un nuovo edificio radicale, il cui centro e punto d'attrazione è un tavolo da degustazione in vetro lungo 8 metri.

Weingut Neumeister

Straden 42 · Straden · Steiermark · Austria · www.neumeister.cc

1998 + 2004
Interior Design: Andreas Burghardt · www.burghardt.co.at
Building Design: Werner Schüttmayr

The declining step-like shape of the production building follows the mountain slope's natural line. At the same time, this displays the winemaking process: the grapes are delivered to the upper section, with the other production stages being located in the building's lower sections.

Die treppenartige Abstufung des Produktionsgebäudes folgt dem natürlichen Hangverlauf. Gleichzeitig bildet es aber auch den Herstellungsprozess des Weines ab: Im oberen Teil werden die Trauben angeliefert, die weiteren Arbeitsschritte finden in den darunter liegenden Gebäudeteilen statt.

Le dégradé en forme d'escalier du bâtiment de production suit la pente naturelle du versant. Il illustre en même temps le processus de production du vin : le raisin est livré dans la partie supérieure, puis les étapes suivantes du travail sont effectuées dans les parties inférieures du bâtiment.

La nivelación parecida a unas escaleras del edificio de la producción continúa el perfil natural de la pendiente. Al mismo tiempo, sin embargo, refleja también el proceso de elaboración del vino: en la parte superior se descargan las uvas y los siguientes pasos se desarrollan en los niveles inferiores.

Il terrazzamento dell'edificio adibito alla produzione segue l'andamento naturale del pendio. Al contempo rappresenta però anche il processo produttivo del vino: nella parte superiore viene consegnata l'uva, mentre le fasi di lavorazione successive si svolgono negli ambienti sottostanti.

Weingut Schützenhof

Weinberg 159 · Deutsch Schützen · Burgenland · Austria · www.schuetzenhof.cc

2004
Pichler & Traupmann Architekten
www.pxt.at

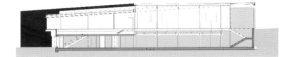

The elegant new building with its generous glass surfaces demonstrates a conscious move away from traditional forms and construction materials in a rural setting. With a view over the vineyards, the wine tasting is in a "showroom" with generous glazing and where the Barrique barrels are also stored.

Der elegante Neubau mit seiner großzügigen Verglasung zeigt eine bewusste Abkehr von den traditionellen Formen und Materialien des Bauens im ländlichen Raum. Die Verkostung des Weines mit Blick über die Weinberge findet in einem großzügig verglasten „Showroom" statt, in dem auch die Barriquefässer lagern.

Avec son vitrage généreux, le nouveau bâtiment élégant indique un abandon volontaire des formes et des matériaux de construction traditionnels dans l'espace rural. La dégustation du vin avec vue sur les vignes se fait dans un « showroom » généreux et vitré dans lequel les barriques sont également stockées.

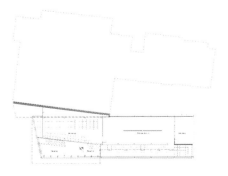

La elegante nueva construcción con su generoso acristalado muestra un alejamiento consciente de las formas y los materiales tradicionales de la construcción rural. La degustación del vino con vistas sobre los viñedos se realza en un "showroom" ampliamente acristalado en el que también se almacenar las barricas.

L'elegante nuova costruzione con le ampie superfici vetrate è espressione del consapevole distacco dalle forme e materiali tradizionali dell'architettura rurale. Le degustazioni dei vini si tengono in uno "showroom" in cui si trovano anche le botti in rovere e da cui si possono ammirare i vigneti.

Weinkulturhaus

Hauptplatz 20 · Gols · Burgenland · Austria · www.weinkulturhaus.at

2003
Interior Design: i-arch Michael Maier · www.i-arch.at
Building Design: Eberstaller & Co

A winemakers' cooperative presents its wines in the oldest building in the wine village of Gols. In the interior of the carefully restored building, the architects created a modern, attractive ambience, where the old and new building elements form a harmonious whole.

Im ältesten Gebäude des Weinortes Gols präsentieren die Winzer gemeinsam ihre Weine. In den Innenräumen des sorgsam restaurierten Baus schufen die Architekten ein modernes, attraktives Ambiente, im dem alte und neue Bausubstanz eine harmonische Verbindung eingehen.

Les vignerons présentent ensemble leurs vins dans le plus ancien bâtiment des terres vinicoles de Gols. Dans les pièces intérieures de la construction restaurée avec soin, les architectes ont créé une ambiance moderne et attrayante grâce à laquelle la substance ancienne et la substance nouvelle de l'édifice se marient harmonieusement.

En el edificio más antiguo del pueblo vinícola Gols los vitivinicultores presentan juntos sus vinos. En los espacios del interior de este edificio cuidadosamente restaurado, los arquitectotes crearon un ambiente moderno y atractivo en el que los elementos antiguos y nuevos de la construcción se unen con armonía.

Nell'edificio più antico di Gols i viticoltori presentano tutti insieme i loro vini. Nei locali della costruzione accuratamente restaurata gli architetti hanno creato un ambiente moderno e attraente, in cui la struttura antica e quella nuova si coniugano armoniosamente.

AXA Winery in Mezőzombor

Diznókő dűlő · Mezőzombor · Tokaj · Hungary · www.disznoko.hu

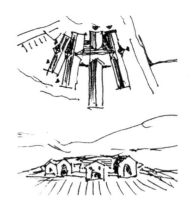

1995
Ekler Architectural Ltd.
www.ekler-architect.hu

The winery consists of three, separate building complexes. The oldest part of the estate dates back to the 19th Century as a Classicist structure, which is still used today as a restaurant; the production and cellar facilities are in the new, finger-shaped structure of the main building. The third building—an unusual, wooden circular construction—serves as a depot for tractors and machines.

Das Weingut besteht aus drei unabhängigen Gebäudekomplexen. Der älteste Teil der Anlage wurde im 19. Jahrhundert als klassizistischer Bau errichtet und wird heute als Restaurant genutzt; im neuen Hauptgebäude mit seiner fingerartigen Struktur befinden sich Produktions- und Kelleranlagen. Der dritte Bau, eine ungewöhnliche hölzerne Rundkonstruktion, dient als Unterstand für Traktoren und Maschinen.

Le domaine viticole est composé de trois complexes indépendants. La plus ancienne partie est une construction néoclassique construite au 19ème siècle et sert aujourd'hui de restaurant ; avec sa structure digitale, le nouveau bâtiment principal héberge les installations de production et les caves. Le troisième édifice, construction ronde en bois et inhabituelle, sert d'abri pour les tracteurs et les machines.

La explotación vinícola esta compuesta por tres complejos independientes de edificios. La parte más antigua data del siglo XIX y es un edificio clasicista que hoy alberga el restaurante; en el nuevo edificio principal, con su estructura con forma de dedo, se encuentran las instalaciones de producción y la bodega. La tercera construcción, de madera y con una forma redonda poco habitual, se emplea como almacén para tractores y maquinaria.

La tenuta è composta da tre complessi indipendenti. La parte più antica, in stile classicistico, risale all'Ottocento ed è adibita a ristorante. Il nuovo edificio principale, con una struttura a forma di dita, ospita gli impianti di produzione e le cantine, mentre il terzo edificio, un'insolita costruzione di legno a pianta circolare, serve da rimessa per trattori e macchine agricole.

Weingut Alois Lageder

Tòr Löwengang · Grafengasse 9 · Margreid · Südtirol · Italy · www.lageder.com

1996
abram & schnabl architekten
www.abram-schnabl.com

The new extension is harmoniously integrated into the building's historical sections. Special emphasis was placed on an ecological construction method and energy-saving operation. An exposed cliff wall supports the natural ventilation system in the wine cellars, whilst solar panels supply hot water and electricity.

Der Neubau fügt sich harmonisch an die historischen Gebäudeteile an. Besonderer Wert wurde auf eine ökologische Bauweise und den energiesparenden Betrieb gelegt. So unterstützt eine naturbelassene Felswand die Klimatisierung der Kellerräume, während Solarkollektoren die Kellerei mit Warmwasser und Elektrizität versorgen.

La nouvelle construction se joint harmonieusement aux parties historiques du bâtiment. Un mode de construction écologique et une utilisation permettant d'économiser de l'énergie ont été privilégiés. C'est la raison pour laquelle une paroi en roche non traitée contribue de manière naturelle à la climatisation des caves, tandis que des capteurs solaires alimentent la cave en eau chaude et en électricité.

El nuevo edificio se adapta de forma armoniosa a las construcciones históricas. Se dio especial valor a una forma ecológica de cultivo y a una explotación de bajo consumo energético. Así, una pared de roca natural contribuye de una forma natural a la climatización de las bodegas, mientras que los colectores solares suministran agua caliente y electricidad.

La nuova costruzione si integra in modo armonioso nel complesso storico della tenuta. Si è data particolare importanza all'utilizzazione di materiali biologici e alla creazione di una struttura a basso consumo energetico: una parete rocciosa naturale, ad esempio, contribuisce alla climatizzazione delle cantine, mentre l'approvvigionamento idrico ed elettrico è garantito da collettori solari.

MANINCOR

St. Josef am See 4 · Kaltern · Südtirol · Italy · www.manincor.de

2004
Angonese, Boday, Köberl

The modern wine cellars at this traditional winery are only visible due to a few access routes and buildings above ground—the historical listed building and gentle aspect of the landscape are maintained almost untouched. Special organic substances were added to the exposed concrete of the subterranean construction, so that over time the surfaces should take on the same color as the vineyard's walls nearby.

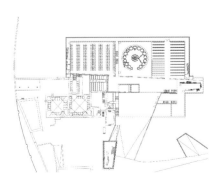

La moderna bodega de esta explotación tradicional sólo se deja ver a través de pocos accesos y por los edificios de la superficie; la construcción histórica y el sensible paisaje se han conservado casi totalmente. El hormigón de la construcción subterránea fue recubierto con sustancias orgánicas especiales que, con el tiempo, deben dotar a los muros del color del entorno.

Die moderne Kelleranlage des Traditionsweingutes tritt nur durch wenige Zufahrten und oberirdische Bauten in Erscheinung, der historische Altbau und das sensible Landschaftsbild bleiben nahezu unverändert erhalten. Dem Sichtbeton des unterirdischen Bauwerks wurden spezielle organische Substanzen zugesetzt, wodurch die Oberflächen nach und nach die Farbe der Weinbergsmauern in der Umgebung annehmen sollen.

La cave moderne du domaine viticole traditionnel ne montre à l'extérieur que quelques bâtiments construits en surface et quelques voies d'accès. Le bâtiment historique ancien et le paysage sensible n'ont quasiment pas été modifiés. Le béton visible du bâtiment souterrain a été revêtu de substances organiques spéciales grâce auxquelles les surfaces devraient prendre peu à peu les couleurs des murs des vignes de la région.

Delle moderne cantine di quest'azienda di lunga tradizione si vedono soltanto alcuni accessi e le costruzioni non interrate: l'edificio storico e la zona circostante, ad elevata sensibilità paesaggistico-naturalistica, sono praticamente immutati. Al cemento a vista della copertura della struttura interrata sono state aggiunte delle speciali sostanze organiche per accelerare il viraggio, cosicché presto il suo colore si avvicinerà sempre più a quello dei muretti dei vigneti circostanti.

Petra

Località San Lorenzo Alto, 131 · Suvereto · Tuscany · Italy · www.petrawine.it

2003
Mario Botta Architetto
www.botta.ch

The distinctive feature of this winery is its strictly geometrical architectural language— a beveled rotunda flanked by side wings. The artificial shape is supposed to symbolize the complex technical production process, the use of local natural stone, on the other hand, highlights the wine's intimate connection to the surrounding landscape.

Seine streng geometrische Architektursprache – eine angeschnittene Rotunde, die von zwei Seitenflügeln flankiert wird – ist das besondere Merkmal dieses Weingutes. Die artifizielle Form soll den aufwendigen technischen Produktionsprozess symbolisieren, die Verwendung von lokalem Naturstein hingegen verdeutlicht die enge Verbindung des Weines mit der umgebenden Landschaft.

Son style architectural strictement géométrique (une rotonde incomplète flanquée de deux ailes) est le signe particulier de ce domaine viticole. La forme artificielle est censée symboliser le processus technique et complexe de la production ; l'utilisation de la pierre locale naturelle démontre en revanche le lien étroit du vin avec le paysage environnant.

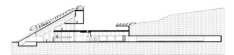

Su estricto lenguaje arquitectónico, una rotonda cortada flanqueada por dos alas laterales, es el elemento característico de esta explotación vinícola. La forma artificial pretende simbolizar el complicado proceso técnico de producción mientras que el empleo de piedra natural local señala hacia la estrecha relación del vino con su entorno.

Il linguaggio architettonico prettamente geometrico – un cilindro sezionato da un piano inclinato e affiancato da due bracci laterali – costituisce la particolare caratteristica di questa tenuta. La forma artificiale simboleggia l'impegnativo processo tecnico di produzione del vino, mentre l'impiego di pietra naturale locale sottolinea lo stretto legame tra il vino e il paesaggio circostante.

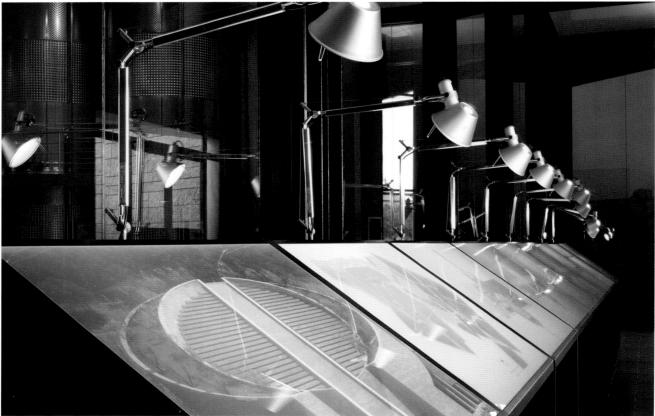

Dornier Wines

Blaauwklippen Road · Stellenbosch · South Africa · www.dornierwines.co.za

2003
Christoph Dornier
Malherbe + Rust Architects

The unusual building adopts elements of classical industrial architecture due to its materials—red brick, glass and metal. In contrast, the rolling roof areas and façades are more reminiscent of the shape of a fish. The nearby mountainous landscape is reflected in a large area of water in front of the building.

Der ungewöhnliche Bau greift durch seine Materialien – roter Backstein, Glas und Metall – Elemente der klassischen Industriearchitektur auf. Die geschwungenen Dachflächen und Fassaden hingegen erinnern eher an die Form eines Fischs. In einer großen Wasserfläche vor dem Gebäude spiegelt sich die umgebende Berglandschaft.

Avec des matériaux comme la brique rouge, le verre et le métal, la construction inhabituelle reprend des éléments de l'architecture industrielle classique. Les surfaces arquées du toit et les façades rappellent en revanche plutôt la forme d'un poisson. Le paysage de montagne environnant se reflète dans une grande étendue d'eau située devant le bâtiment.

Esta insólita construcción retoma a través de sus materiales, ladrillo rojo, cristal y metal, los elementos de la arquitectura industrial clásica. En cambio, las superficies curvas de los tejados y las fachadas recuerdan la forma de un pez. En una gran superficie de agua delante del edificio se reflejan las montañas circundantes.

Con i suoi materiali (mattoni, vetro e metallo) quest'insolita costruzione riprende elementi dell'architettura industriale tradizionale, mentre le facciate e i tetti curvi ricordano piuttosto la forma di un pesce. Le montagne circostanti si riflettono in un grande specchio d'acqua antistante l'edificio.

Amisfield Winery

10 Lake Hayes Road, RD 1 · Queenstown · Central Otago · New Zealand · www.amisfield.co.nz

2002
Warren and Mahoney
www.wam.co.nz

The winery's architecture accentuates forms and materials that are typical of the region. This is how the estate perfectly integrates into the landscape. Taking a closer look, the buildings' carefully designed details reveal a contemporary, almost minimalist touch, which is consistently carried through in elegant interiors.

Die Architektur des Weingutes greift regional typische Formen und Materialien auf. Dadurch fügt es sich perfekt in die Landschaft ein. Auf den zweiten Blick offenbaren die sorgfältig gestalteten Details des Gebäudes einen zeitgemäßen, beinahe minimalistischen Ansatz, der sich in den eleganten Innenräumen konsequent fortsetzt.

L'architecture du domaine viticole s'inspire de formes et de matériaux typiques de la région. Il se fond ainsi parfaitement dans le paysage. Lorsque l'on y regarde de plus près, les détails du bâtiment réalisés avec soin mettent en évidence une approche contemporaine, presque minimaliste, qui se poursuit avec cohérence dans les élégantes pièces intérieures.

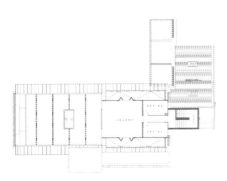

La arquitectura de la explotación agrícola retomas las típicas formas regionales y los materiales. Estos elementos permiten la perfecta integración de las instalaciones en el paisaje. Mirando más detenidamente se descubren los detalles del edificio, de un estilo moderno y casi minimalista, que continúan de forma consecuente en los elegantes espacios interiores.

L'architettura della tenuta riprende forme e materiali tipici della regione, inserendosi alla perfezione nel paesaggio. Ad uno sguardo più attento i curati dettagli dell'edificio svelano un approccio avanguardistico, quasi minimalista, che trova la sua coerente prosecuzione negli eleganti interni.

Peregrine

Kawarau Gorge Road, RD 1 · Queenstown · Central Otago · New Zealand · www.peregrinewines.co.nz

2003
Architecture Workshop Ltd.
www.archwksp.co.nz

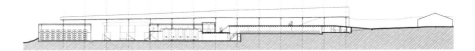

A long, expansive and transparent roof is visible from a quite a distance as an indicator of winemaking and cellar facilities below ground. On the one hand, the style is meant to accentuate horizontal layers of local slate, on the other hand, you are reminded of the wings of a bird—after all, the winery is named after the peregrine falcon.

Ein lang gestrecktes transparentes Dach markiert als weithin sichtbares Zeichen die unterirdischen Produktions- und Kellereianlagen. Dabei soll es einerseits die horizontale Schichtung des lokalen Schiefergesteins aufgreifen, andererseits aber auch an die Flügel eines Vogels erinnern – schließlich ist der Wanderfalke Namensgeber des Weingutes.

Visible de loin, le toit transparent étiré en longueur indique l'emplacement des installations de production et des caves souterraines. Il fait d'un côté allusion à la stratification horizontale de l'ardoise locale et il rappelle également d'un autre côté les ailes d'un oiseau : c'est en effet le faucon pèlerin qui a donné son nom au domaine viticole.

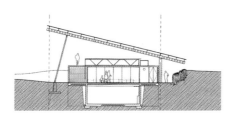

Un tejado alargado y transparente indica de forma visible que debajo de la tierra se encuentran las instalaciones de producción y la bodega. Por un lado refleja la horizontalidad de las capas de pizarra local y, por otro, evoca también el ala de un pájaro y es que el halcón peregrino da nombre a esta explotación vinícola.

Un lungo tetto trasparente, visibile da lontano, contrassegna gli impianti di produzione sotterranei e le cantine. Da un lato riprende la stratificazione orizzontale dell'ardesia locale, dall'altro ricorda anche le ali di un uccello – il falco pellegrino dà in fin dei conti il nome alla tenuta.

Evelyn County Estate

55 Eltham - Yarra Glen Road · Kangaroo Ground · Victoria · Australia · www.evelyncountyestate.com.au

2001
harmer architecture pty. ltd.
www.harmer.com.au

The building located above the vineyards is primarily for sales and wine tasting, though it is used, too, as a restaurant and gallery. Glass surfaces at the sides as well as a horizontal row of windows offer customers and guests a panoramic view across the unique cultural landscape of the Yarra Valley.

Das oberhalb der Weinberge gelegene Gebäude dient in erster Linie dem Verkauf und der Verkostung der Weine, wird aber auch als Restaurant und Galerie genutzt. Seitliche Glasflächen sowie ein horizontales Fensterband bieten Kunden und Gästen eine weite Aussicht über die einzigartige Kulturlandschaft des Yarra Valley.

Le bâtiment situé au-dessus des vignes est destiné en premier lieu à la vente et à la dégustation des vins, mais il sert également de restaurant et de galerie. Les surfaces latérales en verres ainsi que la bande de fenêtres horizontale offrent aux clients et aux visiteurs une vue imprenable sur le paysage culturel unique de la Yarra Valley.

El edificio, situado por encima de las viñas, sirve en primer lugar para la venta y la degustación de los vinos, aunque también se emplea como restaurante y galería. Las superficies laterales acristaladas y el ventanal ofrecen a los clientes y a los huéspedes una amplia vista sobre el paisaje único del Yarra Valley.

L'edificio, che sovrasta i vigneti, è adibito in primo luogo alla degustazione e vendita dei vini, ma funge anche da ristorante e galleria. Superfici laterali vetrate e una fascia di finestre offrono a clienti e ospiti un ampio panorama del singolare paesaggio culturale della Yarra Valley.

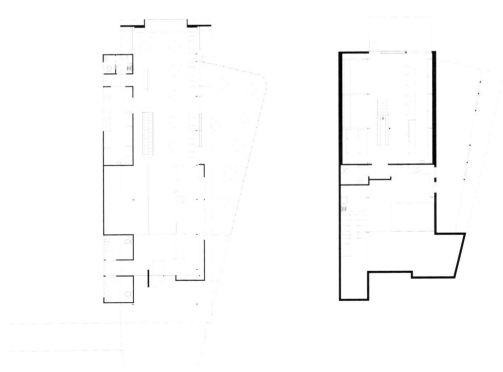

Lerida Estate

The Vineyards · 2581 Lake George · New South Wales · Australia · www.leridaestate.com

2003
Glenn Murcutt

The winery's architecture was perfectly a-dapted to requirements of the winemaking process: production follows a linear process through the entire building—from delivery of the grapes to display and wine sales. The building's deliberate simplicity, almost an industrial design, gains special charm due to its openness and lightness.

Die Architektur des Weingutes wurde perfekt auf die Bedürfnisse des Produktionsablaufs abgestimmt: Die Herstellung verläuft in einem linearen Prozess durch das gesamte Gebäude – von der Anlieferung der Trauben bis zur Präsentation und dem Verkauf des Weines. Die bewusst einfache, fast schon industrielle Gestaltung des Gebäudes gewinnt durch ihre Offenheit und Leichtigkeit einen besonderen Reiz.

L'architecture du domaine viticole a été parfaitement adaptée aux besoins du processus de production. La production traverse tout le bâtiment au cours d'un processus linéaire : de l'arrivée du raisin à la présentation et à la vente du vin. Ouvert et léger, l'agencement du bâtiment, dont la simplicité presque industrielle est volontaire, opère un charme particulier.

La arquitectura de esta explotación vinícola fue adaptada perfectamente a las necesidades del proceso de producción: la elaboración se desarrolla en un proceso lineal a lo largo de todo el edificio; desde el suministro de las uvas hasta la presentación y la venta de los vinos. El diseño conscientemente sencillo y casi industrial del edificio consigue un encanto especial gracias a su carácter abierto y a la sensación de ligereza.

L'architettura dell'azienda è stata concepita rispettando alla perfezione le esigenze delle fasi produttive: la produzione si snoda in un processo lineare attraverso tutto l'edificio – dalla consegna dell'uva alla presentazione e vendita del vino. La concezione dell'edificio, intenzionalmente semplice, ricorda quasi uno stabilimento industriale e acquista un fascino particolare grazie alle strutture aperte e leggere.

Photo Credits

Mission Hill Family Estate Winery	14, 15, 16, 17 Brian Sprout, Paul Warchol
Jackson-Triggs Niagara Estate	9, 18, 19, 20, 21, 22, 23 Tom Arban Photography 2005
Byron Vineyard and Winery	24, 25 Kirk Irvin
Dominus Estate	26 Dominus Estate, 27 Richard Barnes
Quintessa	28 Mark Defeo, 29, 30, 31 Richard Barnes
Roshambo Winery	32 John Sutton, 33 Jaques Ullmann
Juan Alcorta	4, 34, 35, 36, 37, 38, 39 Domecq Bodegas
Bodegas Ysios	4, 40, 41, 42, 43, 44, 45 Domecq Bodegas
Viña Real	46, 47, 48, 49 CVNE S.A.
Domaine Les Aurelles	50, 51 Serge Demailly
Domaine Les Pierre Plantées	52, 53, 54, 55 Serge Demailly
Domaine de Chevalier	56, 57 Domaine de Chevalier
Schloß Wackerbarth	58, 61 Archiv Schloß Wackerbarth,
	59 top, 60 Lothar Sprenger
	59 bottom Michael Miltzow
Weingut am Stein	7, 62, 63, 64, 65 Gerhard Hagen
Weingut Adank	66, 67 Kurt Hauenstein
Wegelin, Scadenagut	68, 69 Ralph Feiner
LOISIUM	6, 70, 71, 72, 73, 74, 75 Robert Herbst
Weingut Lackner-Tinnacher	76, 77, 78, 79 Angelo Kaunat
Weingut Fred Loimer	4, 8, 81, 82, 83 Andreas Burghardt, 80 Weingut Loimer
Weingut Neumeister	10, 84, 85, 86, 87 Jellasitz Kunz Eisenberger
Weingut Schützenhof	88, 89, 90, 91 Paul Ott
Weinkulturhaus	92, 93 Angelo Kaunat
AXA Winery in Mezőzombor	94, 95, 96, 97 Zoltán Boldizár, István Mészáros
Weingut Alois Lageder	98, 99 Alois Lageder, abram & schnabl
MANINCOR	11, 100, 101, 102, 103, 104, 105 archiv bildraum 2004
Petra	3, 106, 107, 108, 109, 110, 111 Miro Zagnoli
Dornier Wines	112, 113, 114, 115, 116, 117 Jeremy Browne
Amisfield Winery	118, 119 Ben Rafferty
Peregrine	5, 120, 121, 122, 123 Patrick Reynolds
Evelyn County Estate	5, 124, 125, 126, 127, 128, 129 meinphoto, Rhiannon Slatter
Lerida Estate	5, 130, 131, 132, 133, 134, 135 Anthony Browell